A PICTURE BOOK OF
John and Abigail Adams

by David A. Adler and Michael S. Adler

illustrated by Ronald Himler

Holiday House / New York

For Michael
—*D. A. A.*

To My Parents
—*M. S. A.*

Text copyright © 2010 by David A. Adler and Michael S. Adler
Illustrations copyright © 2010 by Ronald Himler
All Rights Reserved
HOLIDAY HOUSE is registered in the U.S. Patent and Trademark Office.
Printed and Bound in October 2009 in Johor Bahru, Johor, Malaysia, at Tien Wah Press.
www.holidayhouse.com
First Edition
1 3 5 7 9 10 8 6 4 2

Library of Congress Cataloging-in-Publication Data
Adler, David A.
A picture book of John and Abigail Adams / by David A. Adler and Michael S. Adler ;
illustrated by Ronald Himler. — 1st ed.
p. cm.
Includes bibliographical references.
ISBN 978-0-8234-2007-0 (hardcover)
1. Adams, John, 1735-1826—Juvenile literature. 2. Adams, Abigail, 1744-1818—Pictorial works.
3. Presidents—United States—Biography—Juvenile literature. 4. Presidents' spouses—United States—
Biography—Juvenile literature. I. Adler, Michael S. II. Himler, Ronald, ill. III. Title.
E322.A56 2007
973.4'40922—dc22
[B]
2006050069

John Adams of Massachusetts
was an American patriot, one of
the great men of his time, and
a founder of our nation. His
most trusted adviser, his dearest
friend for more than fifty years,
was his wife, Abigail.

John Adams was born on October 19, 1735, in Braintree (now Quincy), Massachusetts. He was the eldest of John and Susanna Boylston Adams's three sons. His father was a farmer, a deacon in the local church, and a lieutenant in the militia.

Young John Adams enjoyed the outdoors. In the spring and summer, he swam, rolled hoops, sailed toy boats, and flew homemade kites. In the late fall and winter, he sledded, skated, and hunted.

John hoped to become a farmer, but his father had other plans. He taught his son to read. Then he sent John to a local one-room school where he learned to write and do simple arithmetic. Later, John had a private tutor; and at sixteen, he entered Harvard College.

In 1755 John Adams graduated from Harvard intending to become a lawyer. But first he needed to earn some money, so he took a job as a teacher in a one-room schoolhouse in Worcester, Massachusetts. He taught about a dozen students, both boys and girls, and considered his class "the great world in miniature" with "several renowned generals" and several "politicians in petticoats." In 1756 Adams left teaching to study under a local attorney. Two years later he returned to Braintree to practice law.

In 1759 John Adams went with a friend to the home of Reverend William Smith. His friend was courting Mary, the eldest of the three Smith girls. There John met Abigail, the middle sister. She was small, sickly, and just fourteen. He was short, overweight, and difficult. Neither Abigail nor John was greatly impressed with the other.

Abigail Smith was born on November 11, 1744, in Weymouth, Massachusetts, to the Reverend William Smith and Elizabeth Quincy Smith. Her mother's family was among the most prominent in colonial Massachusetts.

John Adams returned often to the Smith house, sometimes with his friend and sometimes to borrow books from Reverend Smith's library. In time, John's and Abigail's feelings changed. He liked that Abigail had opinions of her own. She liked his honesty and wit.

When they couldn't see each other, they wrote teasing, playful letters. He addressed her as "Miss Adorable" and compared her to Aurora, the morning star. She called him "My Friend" and wrote that she thought of him all the time.

John Adams and Abigail Smith married on October 25, 1764, in the Smith home. Then they moved to Braintree and later to Boston. They had five children: Abigail "Nabby," John Quincy, Susanna, Charles, and Thomas. Susanna died shortly after her first birthday.

On March 22, 1765, the British Parliament passed the Stamp Act, a tax in the American colonies on nearly everything written or printed, including pamphlets, newspapers, diplomas, and playing cards. To protest the tax, a Boston mob destroyed British property. John Adams was against the tax, but he didn't approve of what he called such an "atrocious violation of the peace."

In 1766 the Stamp Act was repealed. The next year, however, brought the Townshend Duties—taxes on glass, paper, paint, lead, and tea. With the new taxes came new tensions between England and the colonies.

On March 5, 1770, there was violence in Boston. A large mob surrounded eight British soldiers. They cursed and threw snowballs at the soldiers, who shot into the crowd, killing five, in what became known as the Boston Massacre.

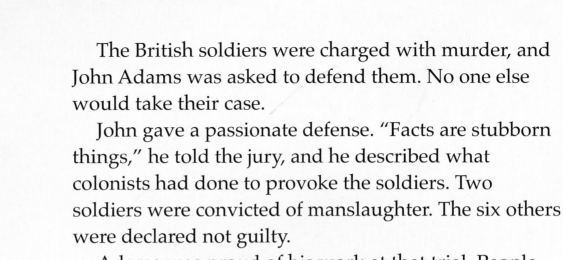

The British soldiers were charged with murder, and John Adams was asked to defend them. No one else would take their case.

John gave a passionate defense. "Facts are stubborn things," he told the jury, and he described what colonists had done to provoke the soldiers. Two soldiers were convicted of manslaughter. The six others were declared not guilty.

Adams was proud of his work at that trial. People respected his integrity. They understood that even British soldiers deserved a proper defense. After the trial, business in Adams's law office was brisk, bringing clients who were among the wealthiest men in Massachusetts.

On March 5, 1770, the same day as the Boston Massacre, Parliament repealed all but one of the Townshend Duties—the tax on tea. On December 16, 1773, in protest, colonists dressed as American Indians dumped 342 chests of English tea into Boston Harbor.

Members of Parliament were furious and closed the port of Boston, which cut off trade and basic supplies. They forced American colonists to feed and house British soldiers. These and other laws became known in America as the Intolerable Acts.

"The flame is kindled," Abigail wrote to a friend. The American colonies were headed toward revolution.

In September 1774 John represented Massachusetts at the Continental Congress in Philadelphia. He and the other delegates protested the Intolerable Acts and resolved to prepare for war.

On April 19, 1775, shots were fired at Lexington and Concord, Massachusetts. The war with Britain had begun.

John Adams returned to Philadelphia for the Second Continental Congress. His family remained in Boston, dangerously close to the battlefield. With more than three hundred miles separating them, John and Abigail wrote each other letters. But these were less playful than the letters they wrote when they were courting.

"The constant roar of the cannon is so distressing that we cannot eat, drink or sleep," Abigail Adams wrote. She also warned her husband to be "generous and favorable" but not to put too much trust in delegates who had slaves.

John Adams served in Congress until February 17, 1778. Then he sailed to France, where he and Benjamin Franklin served as diplomats of the new American nation. John's and Abigail's ten-year-old son, John Quincy, sailed with him. The next year their son Charles joined his father and brother. John Adams and his sons spent most of the next ten years in Europe.

With her husband away, Abigail Adams managed the family's home and money. She missed her husband and sons, but she wrote that she felt "a pleasure in being able to sacrifice my selfish passions to the general good."

The Treaty of Paris in 1783 formally ended the American Revolution. King George III and the British Parliament officially recognized the new nation, the United States of America. In 1784 Abigail and Nabby joined John and the boys in London, where beginning in 1785 John served as America's first ambassador to Great Britain.

By the time they returned home, in March 1788, a new federal Constitution had been drafted. In February 1789 George Washington was elected the nation's first president and John Adams its first vice president. They were reelected in 1793.

While her husband was vice president, Abigail Adams lobbied the new government for equality of education for men and women.

In 1797 George Washington retired to Mount Vernon, Virginia. John Adams narrowly defeated Thomas Jefferson and became the nation's second president. Abigail promised she would be his "fellow Laborer," and she was. "No man ever prospered in the world," she later wrote, "without the consent and cooperation of his wife."

In 1800 the nation's capital was moved from Philadelphia to Washington, D.C. The Adamses were the first to live in the Executive Mansion, soon to be known as the White House.

During Adams's four years as president, the French seized hundreds of American ships and then demanded to be paid just to talk of peace. Adams refused, bringing the two nations to the brink of war. Adams kept the peace, but he lost the support of many Americans. He was defeated by Thomas Jefferson in the presidential election of 1800.

John and Abigail retired to their home in Quincy, Massachusetts. In February 1803 their son John Quincy was elected to the Senate. In 1824 he was elected the nation's sixth president.

Abigail Adams died on October 28, 1818, from typhoid fever. "The tidings of her illness," Reverend Peter Whitney said at her funeral, "were heard with grief in every house."

On July 4, 1826, the fiftieth anniversary of the signing of the Declaration of Independence, John Adams died. Thomas Jefferson, by then a close friend of Adams, died the same day.

"My father had nearly closed the ninety-first year of his life," President John Quincy Adams said of his father, "a life illustrious in the annals of his country and of the world."

John and Abigail are buried side by side in the United First Parish Church in Quincy, Massachusetts.

IMPORTANT DATES

1735   John Adams born in Braintree (now Quincy), Massachusetts, October 19.

1744   Abigail Smith born in Weymouth, Massachusetts, November 11.

1764   Abigail Smith and John Adams marry, October 25.

1770   Boston Massacre, March 5. Adams successfully defends British soldiers.

1773   Boston Tea Party, December 19.

1774, 1775   John Adams is a delegate at First and Second Continental Congresses.

1776   John Adams signs Declaration of Independence.

1778   John Adams joins American diplomatic mission to France.

1784   Abigail Adams joins John in Europe.

1785   John Adams appointed America's first ambassador to Great Britain.

1789   John Adams elected vice president.

1790   John and Abigail Adams move to Philadelphia, then the nation's capital.

1796   John Adams elected president.

1798   French seize American ships, bringing nations close to war.

1800   John and Abigail Adams move to Washington, D.C., the nation's new capital.

1818   Abigail Adams dies, October 28.

1824   John Quincy Adams elected president.

1826   John Adams dies, July 4.

SOURCE NOTES

Each source note includes the first word or words and the last word or words of a quotation and its source. References are to books cited in the Selected Bibliography.

"the great . . . miniature"; "several . . . generals";
    "politicians in petticoats": McCullough, p. 38.

"Miss Adorable"; "My Friend": Akers, p. 15.

"atrocious . . . peace.": McCullough, p. 59.

"Facts are . . . things": McCullough, p. 68.

"The flame is kindled": St. George, p. 26.

"The constant . . . or sleep": Brookhiser, p. 26.

"generous and favorable": Akers, p. 43.

"a pleasure . . . general good.": Akers, p. 73.

"fellow Laborer": Akers, p. 143.

"No man . . . of his wife.": Akers, p. 189.

"The tidings . . . house.": McCullough, p. 624.

"My father . . . the world.": Smith, vol. II, p. 1137.

SELECTED BIBLIOGRAPHY

Adams, James Truslow. *The Adams Family*. New York: Literary Guild, 1930.

Akers, Charles W. *Abigail Adams: An American Woman*. Boston: Little, Brown, 1980.

Brookhiser, Richard. *America's First Dynasty: The Adamses, 1735–1918*. New York: Free Press, 2002.

Butterfield, L. H., Marc Friedlaender, and Mary-Jo Kline , eds. *The Book of Abigail and John: Selected Letters of the Adams Family 1762–1784*. Cambridge, MA: Harvard University Press, 1975.

McCullough, David. *John Adams*. New York: Simon & Schuster, 2001.

St. George, Judith. *John and Abigail Adams: An American Love Story*. New York: Holiday House, 2001.

Smith, Page. *John Adams*. 2 vols. New York: Doubleday & Company, Inc., 1962.

Whitney, Janet. *Abigail Adams*. Boston: Little, Brown and Company, 1947.

RECOMMENDED WEBSITES

www.whitehouse.gov/history/presidents/ja2.html

www.americanpresident.org/history/johnadams

www.ushistory.org/declaration/signers/adams_j.htm

www.whitehouse.gov/history/firstladies/aa2.html

AUTHORS' NOTES

When the Gregorian calendar was adopted in 1752, John Adams's birthday was changed to October 30. Similarly, Abigail Adams's birthday was changed to November 22.

At Harvard College, students were seated by social rank. John was seated fourteenth in a class of twenty-four.

There were two trials following the Boston Massacre. At the first, with John Adams defending him, the soldiers' superior officer, Captain Thomas Preston, was found not guilty.

Adams and Jefferson are the only two future presidents to have signed the Declaration of Independence.

At the time of the first presidential election, each elector was to cast two votes for the president. The person with the most votes became president and the runner-up became vice president. Although John Adams technically ran for president, he was well aware that Washington would be chosen.